An eighteenth-century coach – still a rarity over a hundred years after the first public coaches. The roof was curved, but some brave passengers rode on top at half fare. Eventually coachbuilders made the roof flat and added safety rails and seats. Steel springs of a primitive kind – they often broke – were added after 1750 and glass windows replaced leather curtains. Six horses drew the coach and a postillion rode the nearside leader (the leading horse on the left). It was he who guided the horses, while the coachmen controlled the back four.

The coachman's box seat was separate from the body of the coach and had no springs. Some people feared he would fall asleep if his seat were made more comfortable. The huge basket at the back was for luggage, but passengers sometimes travelled in it also.

THE EDINBURGH STAGE-COACH, for the better Accommodation of Paſſengers, will be altered to a new genteel Two-end Glaſs Machine, hung on Steel Springs, exceeding light and eaſy, to go in ten Days in Summer and twelve in Winter, to ſet out the firſt Tueſday in March, and continue it from Hoſea Eaſtgate's, the Coach and Horſes in Dean-ſtreet, Soho, LONDON, and from John Somervell's in the Canon gate, Edinburgh, every other Tueſday, and meet at Burrow-bridge on Saturday Night, and ſet out from thence on Monday Morning, and get to London and Edinburgh on Friday. In the Winter ſet out from London and Edinburgh every other Monday Morning, and to get to Burrow-bridge on Saturday Night; and to ſet out from thence on Monday Morning, and get to London and Edinburgh on Saturday Night. · Paſſengers to pay as uſual. Perform'd, if God permits, by your dutiful Servant,   HOSEA EASTGATE.
    Care is taken of ſmall Parcels, paying according to their Value.

Hosea Eastgate's advertisement for his New Glass Machine to Edinburgh, 1754

Coaching bills advertising public services gave a rosy picture of stagecoach travel. A London–Chester coach in the seventeenth century was supposed to take four days, but we can be certain it never kept to time. An Exeter coach was supposed to reach London in four days in 1658, but fifty years later its usual time was six or seven days. Coachmasters looked on the bright side. At the end of their timetables announcing arrival times of the coach, they added the phrase, 'If God Permits'. Most of the time, God did not.

Post coach – a smaller (four passengers at most), lighter coach of the late eighteenth century. Rich families sometimes owned travelling coaches of this kind, and some were used on public services, usually on short routes. It was on this type of coach that the art of driving 'four-in-hand' (the driver controlling all four horses individually) developed.

2 THE MAIL

In 1782 the post was so slow that many people sent their letters by stagecoach, although that was illegal (only the Post Office was – and is – allowed to deliver letters). John Palmer, a theatre manager from Bath with a good head for business, produced a scheme for faster delivery of the mail by special mail-coaches, with relays of good horses and an armed guard riding with the coachman. The Post Office, which has always been very slow to take up new ideas, did not like Palmer's scheme, but the prime minister, William Pitt, insisted that it should be tried.

Palmer's first mail-coach left Bristol at 4 p.m. on 2 August 1784, stopped at Bath eighty minutes later, and arrived at the G.P.O. in London at 9 a.m. the next morning. Not only was it twice as fast as the postboy, it was slightly faster than the quickest Bristol–London stagecoach.

The coach used for this first run was an ordinary light coach, or post coach, but in 1787 John Besant designed a new vehicle which became the model for all mail-coaches. It was built by Vidler of Millbank, Besant's partner, who built and serviced all mail-coaches for the next forty years. Unlike stage-coaches, which were often brightly painted and carried advertisements for their proprietors, the mail-coaches were dignified and sombre, painted maroon and black. They all looked exactly alike except that each coach had the town it travelled to neatly stencilled in gold on the door.

Besant's model mail-coach had the boot built into the body of the coach – the old jogging basket at the back disappeared. At the front, the coachman's box seat was still separated from the body; it was not built-in until after 1803, when the mail-coach approached its final form. The guard sat at the back, his feet planted firmly on the iron lid of the boot which contained the mailbags. No outside passengers were allowed at the back, so that the guard had a free field of fire if highwaymen attacked – though in fact they almost never attacked a mail-coach.

Only the guard was a Post Office employee. The coach was owned by the maker and hired out at so much per mile. Horses were hired by the mile from innkeepers, who were often also postmasters, along the route; they paid the coachman's wages and made their profit from passengers' fares. The rate for hiring horses was no higher than the rate for the old mounted postboys, and because the new system was much more efficient, the Post Office was able to raise postage rates. Profits zoomed up.

John Palmer

Until 1784 the mail in England was carried by postboys on horseback. Although they were called 'boys', many of them were elderly men and a few, in out-of-the-way places, were women.

Their pay was low and they were unreliable. The average speed of the post was only $3\frac{1}{2}$ miles an hour, and delays were frequent. On a cold and rainy day it was tempting to warm the blood with a jug of gin, and some postboys were not above squeezing the packets they carried to see if they could hear the crisp crackle of banknotes. The Post Office advised people sending money by the post to cut the notes in half and send them separately. When they heard that the first lot had arrived, they could safely send the matching halves. Even if the postboy were honest, he might be held up by highwaymen, and one un-armed boy or old man did not stand much chance against two or three rogues with clubs or pistols.

In the days when Queen Victoria was a young girl, one of the great sights of London, like the Changing of the Guard, was the departure of the mails from the G.P.O. in St Martin's-le-Grand.

Mail-coaches travelled at night (during the next day too, of course, if going far enough), and they all left London together at eight in the evening. Throughout the night they would be rattling briskly north, south, east, and west, their oil-lamps casting a glow on the road ahead and warning all other road-users to make way for His Majesty's Mail. Besides the mail, they also brought the latest news from the capital. It was the mail-coaches, decked with laurel leaves for victory, which brought the news of Waterloo to the towns and villages of rural England in 1815.

The dramatic improvement in the speed of coach travel would have been impossible without better roads, but it was the mail-coach that introduced people to the idea of really fast travel by coach. Stagecoaches soon followed the mail's example and tightened up their schedules. In fact, some of the crack long-distance stagecoaches of the 1820s and 1830s equalled the mail's time, though on the whole the mails were slightly faster than stagecoaches (and charged slightly higher fares). The table below shows the ever-increasing speeds of coaches on two main roads between 1730 and 1830. (The eighteenth-century coaches stopped overnight, so their actual travelling time was less than the figures suggest.)

Coach Journey Times, from London

	To Newcastle	To Manchester
1730	12 days	
1754	9 days	$4\frac{1}{2}$ days
1770	5 days	3 days
1780		2 days
1790	$2\frac{1}{2}$ days	
1821		26 hours
1825	36 hours	18 hours
1830	30 hours	

3 THE PERFECTION OF THE COACH-AND-FOUR

By 1830 coaches had reached their final form. Mail-coaches and the better stagecoaches were now built on much the same lines. Compared with the old-fashioned coach of the eighteenth century (see no. 1), which could still be seen on country roads, the modern vehicle was neater, more solid, lighter, and closer to the ground. It was built in one piece, with the coachman's box and the boot (replacing the old basket) joined to the main body. The roof was flat and had decent seats and guard rails: travelling 'outside' might be cold and uncomfortable, but it was no longer downright dangerous. There was room for seven outside passengers (less on a mail) and six, or sometimes four, inside. Every coach was licensed to carry a fixed number of passengers, but at busy times it might cram more than the legal number on board.

Large wheels made the coach easier to draw, but they also raised it dangerously high from the ground. In fact, coaches were always rather top-heavy; the 1830 coach was lower than earlier models thanks to better springs and a lighter perch (the beam that ran between the axles). The front wheels were smaller than the rear because they had to turn without locking against the body, which was likely to overturn the coach.

The chain that hung below the coach could be fastened to a rear wheel, jamming it, when the coach was going down a steep hill. Except for this primitive device, most public coaches had no brakes. The driver relied on the strength of the wheel horses and his own skill to stop the coach running away on a downward slope.

The coach was drawn by a team of four horses controlled by the driver on the box. In an emergency – a heavy snowfall or muddy hill – a third pair might be 'put to' with a rider on the nearside leader (because not more than four horses could be controlled from the box). But by 1830 the main roads were so good that four horses were the normal rule, and 'four-in-hand' driving became an art.

The horses were the most expensive item in running a coach. A decent coach horse cost about £30 to buy and about £4 a month to keep, but its

working life, on a fast coach, was only about three years – cruelly short compared with a brewery dray horse, which works at least seven years. The average stage covered by each team of horses was eight to ten miles, and the wise proprietor did not make any team work every day of the week. But some teams covered 'both sides of the ground' (meaning 'there and back') in the same day.

Fortunately, coach horses did not need any special qualities as long as their stamina was good. A blind horse could work perfectly well in harness, and a horse with a nasty temper, or some bad habit which made it impossible to ride, would often settle down as one of a team. Slightly different qualities were needed in leaders (the front pair) and wheelers. The wheelers did the hardest work and had the tough job of holding the coach back when going downhill; they were usually the stronger pair.

The more dashing leaders had to be reliable; if a wheeler broke down, the other three would 'carry' him, but if one of the leaders cracked a nasty tangle was the likely result.

It was important that the horses in each pair should be well matched. Different-sized horses paired together would make progress uneven, and there were more subtle points to look for. A horse that held his head high, for example, would not be paired with one that held it low; a horse that bored to the right would not be placed on the nearside, where he would interfere with his partner. Horses are not machines and, like people, they have individual characters and odd little habits. Good coachmen and horsekeepers never forgot that. There used to be a grey leader stabled in Hounslow which gave endless trouble until a coachman thought of putting caps on his ears. After that he went perfectly.

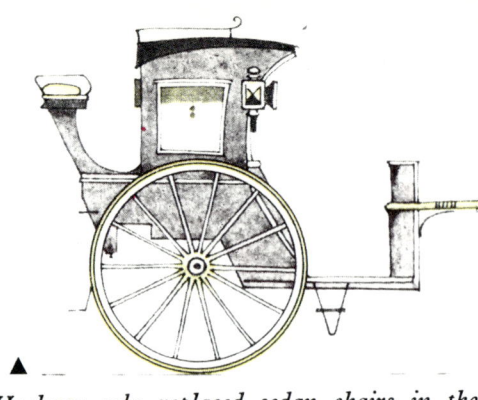

beautifully decorated, a sedan chair was simply a large box with a seat inside and two carrying shafts along the sides. The front opened like a door and the roof could be lifted so the person inside could stand up without banging his head. For some reason London 'chairmen' were nearly always Irish. They were a rough and independent lot, and it was not wise to argue over the fare.

Ladies and gentlemen who wished to get about the narrow streets of an eighteenth-century city without fouling their shoes or jostling with the crowd took a sedan chair. Though sometimes

▲

Hackney cabs replaced sedan chairs in the nineteenth century. They were quicker, and probably cheaper: one man and one old, broken-down, probably half-starved horse cost less than two fit Irishmen. The first hackney carriage ('hackney' means 'for hire') appeared in London early in the seventeenth century, and by 1832 there were at least 1,200 of them. That number of licences was issued, though there were probably other carriages operating illegally. Some were old private carriages which had grown too old and shabby for their owners, but most of them were specially made as 'cabs'. Many different types could be seen in the London streets in Queen Victoria's reign, some with two huge wheels higher than the roof, some with the driver's seat behind the cab. They were small and narrow, and slipped easily through busy streets.

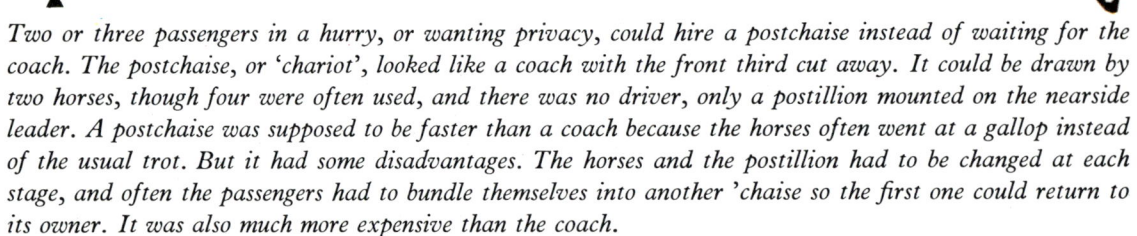

▲

Two or three passengers in a hurry, or wanting privacy, could hire a postchaise instead of waiting for the coach. The postchaise, or 'chariot', looked like a coach with the front third cut away. It could be drawn by two horses, though four were often used, and there was no driver, only a postillion mounted on the nearside leader. A postchaise was supposed to be faster than a coach because the horses often went at a gallop instead of the usual trot. But it had some disadvantages. The horses and the postillion had to be changed at each stage, and often the passengers had to bundle themselves into another 'chaise so the first one could return to its owner. It was also much more expensive than the coach.

The cheapest way to travel before railways were built was by carrier's waggon. Carrying mainly goods and parcels, they ran regularly, like stagecoaches, but much more slowly, sometimes averaging only twenty miles a day. They were drawn by teams of eight horses, sometimes more, and the carrier walked or rode alongside with his long carrier's whip. Because they were so heavy, carriers' waggons could damage road surfaces, especially in wet weather, and to prevent that they were compelled by law to have wheels with very wide rims. The law was unpopular with the carriers because the wide wheels, while they did not carve ruts in the surface, created more friction and made the waggons harder to draw.

4 OTHER WAYS OF TRAVELLING

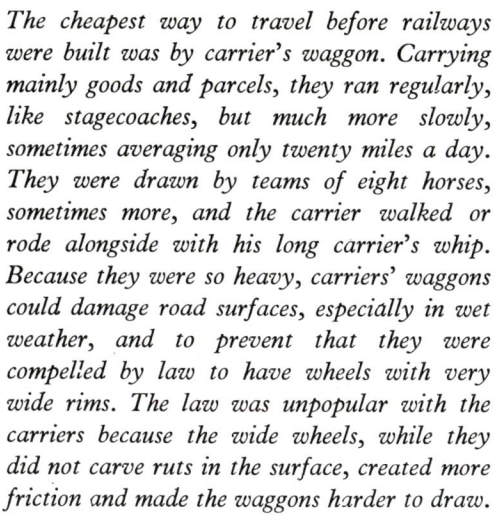

In the country people still often travelled on horseback. Though the coach was quicker, a horse did not need a good road like a coach, and could take short-cuts. By changing horses at 'posting' inns (which also provided coach horses and usually had a postchaise for hire), a long distance could be covered at a fair speed, and in good weather it was a pleasant way to travel. Highway-men were few by 1830, though the cautious rider did not travel alone in lonely places.

In earlier times, all goods that could not be sent by water went by packhorse (see the inn sign in no. 12). Even coal and building stone were once transported in this way. In the early nineteenth century long trains of packhorses could sometimes still be seen winding their way through the wilder parts of the country though they had become a rare sight in the south of England.

The appearance of stagecoaches changed a great deal between the late eighteenth century and the early nineteenth century. In general, they became squarer, more compact and lower. Several developments helped to cause these changes, including smoother roads, better horses, faster travelling and more passengers, but technical improvements were also important, especially Obadiah Elliot's new type of spring. This allowed a much lighter perch, with the body of the coach closer to the ground. At the same time the coachman's box was joined to the coach, which made it more stable, gave the coachman a more comfortable ride (the old, separated box had no springs) and allowed more outside passengers.

The parts of the coach that suffered the hardest wear and were most easily damaged were the wheels and axles. As wheels were made by hand, everything depended on the skill and the accurate eye of the craftsman.

A coach or carriage wheel has three basic parts: the nave (the central hub which receives the axle), spokes, and felloes (the curved segments making up the outer ring of the wheel). The wheelwright began by making the nave, usually of elm wood, on a lathe, and boring the holes for the spokes (twelve or fourteen on a rear wheel, ten or twelve on a front wheel). The spokes were made of oak – torn, not cut, from the timber to avoid splitting – and driven into the nave with a mallet. Then the felloes, usually made of ash and joined together by wooden dowels, were driven into place, and an iron hoop, heated to make it expand, was fitted around the rim. As it cooled it contracted and tightened.

Axles were even more troublesome than wheels, and many attempts were made to invent the perfect axle. The most common type was called the mail axle (because it was first used on mail-coaches). Simply, it was a wrought-iron bar whose 'arms' revolved inside cast-iron boxes driven into the naves of the wheel and lubricated with oil. The mail axle was strong, fairly cheap, and safe – the wheel did not come off if the axle broke at the 'collar'. However, it was not particularly smooth-running. Cases were known of an axle becoming so hot through friction that it set fire to the wheel.

Steel springs of various kinds were first fitted to stagecoaches in the middle of the eighteenth century, but they were not very efficient and often broke. In 1804 a great technical breakthrough was made when Obadiah Elliot invented the elliptical spring, which can still be seen on some vehicles today. Most four-horse coaches used an adaptation called 'Telegraph' springs, named after the stagecoach which had them first.

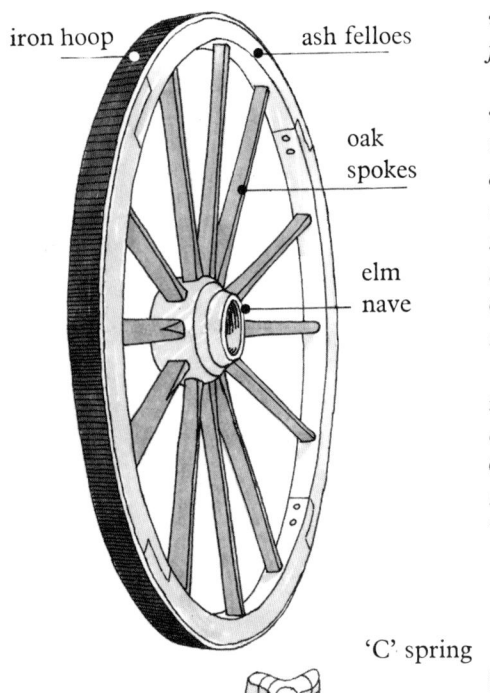

iron hoop   ash felloes

oak spokes

elm nave

'C' spring

elliptical spring

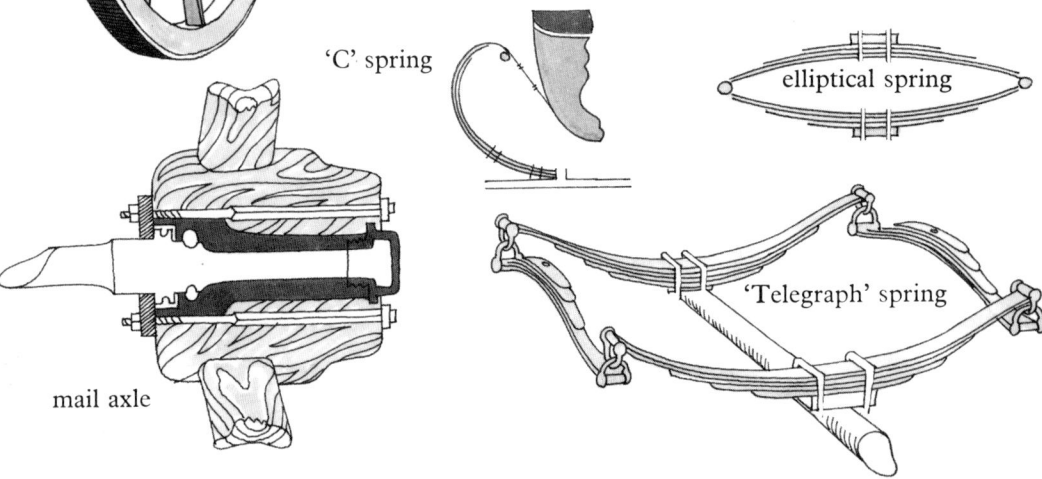

'Telegraph' spring

mail axle

5 BUILDING THE COACH

Coachmaking was a fine craft which required as much knowledge, patience, and skill as furniture-making. In the days when labour, even skilled labour, was cheaper than it is now, an enormous amount of time and care went into the building and decorating of an expensive private carriage on a top-class stagecoach. There were thirty or forty different processes involved in finishing a door panel – painting, smoothing, varnishing, etc. No respectable coachmaker would use less than six or seven coats of varnish, carefully sanding down each one before applying the next.

To run a coaching business demanded plenty of money, not only to keep a good stock of materials but also to pay many different craftsmen: body-makers, carriage-makers, wheelwrights, smiths, painters, and harness-makers. Many other crafts, like lamp-making or lace-making, were also involved in coachbuilding at some stage. A good craftsman could make as much as £5 a week in the coachbuilding trade in the 1830s, but £2 or £3 was the average wage.

Building a coach required the skills of many different craftsmen using hundreds of different tools, but considered as a machine, the coach was a rather simple vehicle: the 'engine' was the horses and the 'controls' were the reins. Stagecoaches carried only two essential pieces of extra equipment: the 'chain' (or 'skid', or 'shoe'), which jammed the back wheel when going down a steep hill, and the lamps – oil-burning on public coaches, candles on private carriages.

▼

Coachmen, like the coaches they drove, changed over the years. When roads were bad and coaches slow, the coach was often drawn by six or eight horses, with a postillion riding the leading horse. The postillion guided the team, and the coachman knew little of the skill of driving 'four-in-hand'. But if not skilful, the old-fashioned coachman had to be strong. Sitting on his hard, jolting box-seat (no springs in those days), he forced the tired horses onward for hours on end, over muddy, rutted roads and up steep, slippery hills. Coming down the hills, he had to hold the horses in check while his top-heavy coach swayed and lurched behind him and the poor horses, after many miles of hard hauling, tried to break away from the weight of the coach pressing upon them.

6 THE COACHMAN

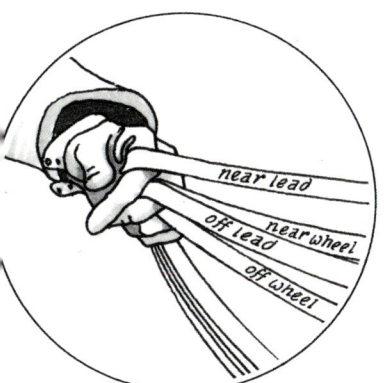

The most important person on a stagecoach was of course the man who drove it – 'coachie', as familiar passengers would call him. On a long-distance stagecoach, the coachman usually drove fifty or sixty miles a day, though some drove much farther.

In spite of the responsibility of his job and the experience and skill that it demanded, the coachman was paid a low wage, sometimes as little as £1 a week (not much more than an unskilled labourer). But on a good road, he might make £5 or £6 a week from tips.

Coachmen had a high opinion of their profession. They could be very snobbish towards poor passengers and scornful of any man who did not know the arts of coachmanship. Coachmen on fashionable coaches were on friendly terms with sporting aristocrats, and tended to behave like aristocrats themselves. At the annual dinner given by Mrs Nelson of the Bull, Aldgate, for her coachmen, the guests called each other not 'Tom' or 'Dick', not even 'Mr Smith' or 'Mr Jones', but, according to the road they drove on, 'Oxford', 'Chelmsford', or 'Dover'.

A very different figure occupied the box of a crack coach in the later, golden age of coaching – the 1820s and 1830s. Fashionable day-coaches on the Brighton or Chelmsford roads were driven by elegant gentlemen in well-brushed top hats and well-cut frock coats with pearl buttons and a posy in the buttonhole. The fashionable coachman would not touch country ale or rough spirits, preferring to drink a glass of sherry or white wine. He was sometimes a real 'gentleman', even a lord, who drove a public coach because he enjoyed it: but the driver of any smart coach was a person of great prestige, admired by stableboys and adored by maidservants up and down the road. He expected, and usually received, an extra-large tip from the passenger who had the honour to share his seat on the box.

The driver of a fast coach was an artist, an expert, who made a difficult job look easy. His hands moved as little as possible: the better the coachman, the less he seemed to be actually doing. His left hand, with the reins passing between the fingers, was held easily just in front of his belt buckle, elbow close to the side. There were four reins for the four horses (see above), and the good coachman never forgot which rein was which any more than a car driver forgets which pedal is the accelerator and which is the brake. If he pulled the wrong rein when he wanted to turn a corner, the coach would very likely end in the ditch. The whip, held in the right hand pointing diagonally forwards, was seldom needed by the kind of coachman who could pick a fly off the ear of the nearside leader.

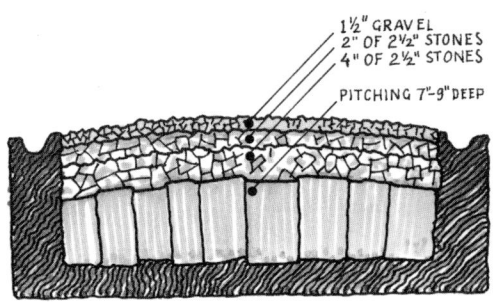

1½" GRAVEL
2" OF 2½" STONES
4" OF 2½" STONES
PITCHING 7"-9" DEEP

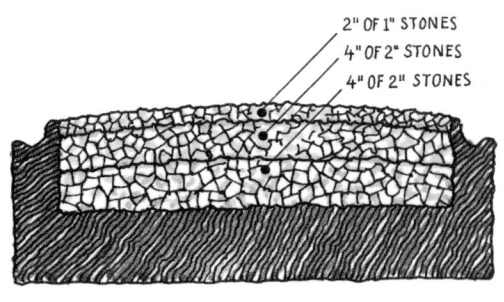

2" OF 1" STONES
4" OF 2" STONES
4" OF 2" STONES

Telford built hundreds of miles of roads in Scotland and reconstructed the London–Holyhead road, the busiest in Britain. He began by careful excavating and levelling. The foundation was made of large, interlocking stones with smaller stones above, and on top of them a layer of coarse gravel. Drains were laid at intervals across the road below the foundations.

McAdam's system was equally good and much less costly. McAdam believed that a road would wear better if it had some 'give' in it. He laid one-inch stones on the prepared soil, with a finer layer on top. The whole surface was only ten inches thick, but it was raised above the general level of the ground and sloped slightly to let the rain run off. McAdam's road-building methods were eventually copied everywhere.

7 MAKING THE ROADS

The golden age of coaching did not begin until the early nineteenth century. Yet coaches could have been built much earlier. After all, the Ancient Egyptians drove about in wheeled carriages, so why did the stagecoach take so long to develop? The chief reason was the dreadful state of the roads. Until the late eighteenth century, the average English road was a muddy lane, winding in a trench through woods, moors and marshes. It was often almost blocked by large stones, fallen trees or floodwater, and it was usually pitted with deep holes and ruts. As late as 1750 people living in Kensington sometimes could not reach Westminster because the roads were impassable. A man who was thrown from his horse near Ipswich in 1769 suffocated in the mud. The ruts in a main road in Lancashire were four feet deep when the traveller Arthur Young measured them in 1770. So the few stage-coaches on the roads in the eighteenth century moved slowly and with difficulty. A journey from Chester to London (180 miles) in 1739 took five days, and at times eight horses were needed to move the coach at all.

A big improvement began with the turnpike system in the eighteenth century. By 1830 about 20,000 miles of British roads (about one-tenth of the total) were turnpikes. But what gave Britain its first really good roads since the days of the Roman Empire were the new methods of road-building carried out by Thomas Telford (1757–1834), the famous engineer who built the Menai Strait suspension bridge, and by J. L. McAdam (1756–1836), from whose name comes the word 'macadamize'.

Certain stretches of road were improved in the eighteenth century by bodies called turnpike trusts. The members of each trust, who included local landowners and justices of the peace, were responsible for rebuilding and maintaining a particular piece of road. In return, they could charge a toll at the 'turnpike' – a pole acting as a barrier across the road. The word 'turnpike' later came to describe the toll-gates that replaced the pole, and then the road itself. A toll-keeper or 'pikeman' was appointed by the trust and a house was built for him next to the toll-gates. (Some can still be seen, now turned into ordinary cottages.) They were nearly always one storey high (the toll-keeper slept on the ground floor as he had to open the gates at night as well).

Toll charges were based on the size of the vehicle, or the number of horses drawing it, or, in the case of goods waggons, the weight – measured by a clumsy type of crane that often broke down and caused long delays. But the mails paid no tolls (except in Scotland), which greatly annoyed the proprietors of stagecoaches.

8 THE GUARD

Guards were first put on mail-coaches to prevent robbery, but they had other duties besides. By 1830 most long-distance coaches, stage as well as mail, carried a guard, although the danger of robbery had almost disappeared.

Compared with the splendid figure of the coachman, the guard of a stagecoach seems a more humble fellow. But on a mail-coach the guard had the most important responsibilities, for he alone was in charge of the mail. Unlike the coachman, he was employed directly by the Post Office, and he wore a magnificent Post Office uniform of red and gold.

Besides looking after parcels and luggage, the guard had the pleasant duty of blowing the horn, which warned postmasters, toll-keepers and other road-users that the coach was coming. It was the guard too who hopped down to put on the chain at the top of a hill, who helped change the horses at each stage, and made sure the coach kept to time.

Coachmen generally drove for fifty or sixty miles, but the guard usually travelled much farther. Some stagecoach guards travelled regularly from London to York, Plymouth or Holyhead (260 miles). No one else in the country covered such long distances so frequently and so fast, and that gave an enterprising guard opportunities to increase his low wages (10s 6d a week for a mail guard). Guards would perform errands in London for people living far away. They might find out if a sick uncle was better, or if a son was happy in his London apprenticeship, and give a first-hand report to the anxious family as fast as a letter could travel. Some guards even acted as newspaper reporters, bringing news of the latest events in the capital to the editor of a local paper in some distant town. Others did a little private trading in articles which could be bought cheap in one part of the country and sold dear in another. Many a goose, salmon, or even a live sheep, made the journey up to London in the guard's care.

▲ *A guard putting the skid-chain on a stagecoach to stop it running on to the horses when descending a steep hill.*

The old coach horn was a straight brass or copper horn, flared at the end and up to three feet long. It was carried in a wickerwork basket near the guard's seat. But in the great age of coaching in the 1820s and 1830s many guards preferred a key bugle – an instrument like a trumpet. On this they could play tunes, and some of them were quite skilful musicians, capable of Italian opera as well as English folk-songs. One guard specialized in imitating the 'moo' of a cow, which he did so well that cattle would come running across the fields as the coach passed. ▼

▲

The first duty of the mail-coach guard was to make sure that the mail arrived safely and on time. On a mail-coach the mail bags were the most important thing; passengers came second. If the coach was delayed by an accident, it was the guard's duty to get the bags to their destination as soon as possible, even if that meant taking one of the coach horses to ride. Most mail guards showed a high sense of duty, and several actually lost their lives while trying to cross a flooded river or force a way through a snowstorm after the coach had been stranded.

The equipment of the mail guard included a box of weapons: blunderbuss, cutlass and pistols. They were more often used to bag a pheasant or rabbit than to repel a highwayman. The guard also had charge of the waybill, a list of the mail bags or other parcels, and a clock, which was locked in a special case and could not be altered by the guard, who had to explain any delay it showed. Guards were responsible for seeing that coaches carried shovels, crow-bars, ropes, and spares to replace or mend broken springs, harness, and other parts.

The mail bags were carried in the boot under the guard's feet. But the boots of coaches sometimes concealed much stranger things: poached game, smuggled brandy, even stolen silver on its way to a 'fence' in London.

9 THE COACHING BUSINESS

The coaching business employed a large number of people, from porters, horsekeepers and postboys to innkeepers, postmasters and proprietors. William Chaplin, the biggest coach proprietor in London, employed about 2,000 people. He had an equal number of horses stabled in London and suburban staging posts, and ran about 200 coaches.

Coach proprietors ordered their coaches from coachbuilders in a style and design they wanted, though some, like Mr Sherman of the Bull and Mouth, owned their own coachbuilding business. Otherwise, most stagecoaches remained the property of the coachbuilder, who kept them in good order and rented them out to the coachmasters at about 3d per mile of the route (there and back). The cost of building a coach was about £140; extra-smart coaches cost more. Several coaches were needed for each route, so the Shrewsbury *Wonder*, or the Manchester *Telegraph*, was not one vehicle but several.

The big coach proprietors in London and major cities were nearly always innkeepers. Most coach services were run by a partnership, consisting of the two proprietors at each end of the route and some (or all) of the men in between who provided the horses at staging posts. Often, the smaller proprietors, or those who 'horsed' the coach without sharing in the business, would double as coachmen, and drive their own teams for a stage or two.

Although fares were high, so were the coach proprietors' expenses. Besides hire of the coach and cost of the horses, they had to pay a tax on the coach, tolls on the turnpikes, wages for the coachmen and various other expenses including – if the coach had an accident – damages to injured passengers. Some of the most fashionable stagecoaches ran at a loss. Their proprietors kept them on the road as an advertisement, and made up the losses on their less glamorous, slow coaches.

Two large items of expenditure were 'horsing' the coach (paying for the hire of horses from innkeepers at each stage) and, much to the anger of the proprietors, government duties, which were calculated on the distance the coach travelled and the number of passengers it was licensed to carry. The cost of tolls on the turnpikes varied, but on a major road like the Great North Road, tolls were likely to be the most expensive single item. By comparison, wages were low. The usual wage for a mail-coach guard was 10s 6d a week. The coachman was paid about twice as much, but both men earned more from tips than wages.

In these accounts for a single journey, the stagecoach is shown to be making a profit of just over 100 per cent. This seems quite a lot, although it had to be divided among several partners. More important, the coach is shown to have a full load of passengers. But it was not likely to be full on every journey. If only half the seats were taken, the coach was hardly covering its costs.

Stagecoach London to Edinburgh (1830) Accounts   *William Chaplin*

Expenses

	£	s	d
Mileage charge (duty)	4	19	3
Hire of coach	4	0	0
Horsing (3d a mile)	4	19	3
Turnpike tolls	6	12	0
Wages & Miscellaneous	12	0	0
	32	10	6

Receipts

	£	s	d
4 Inside Passengers (at £6–15 each)	27	0	0
11 Outside Passengers (at £3–10 each)	38	10	0
	65	10	0

The 'big three' among London coach proprietors were Chaplin, Sherman, and Horne. It was said that Chaplin's gross income was half a million pounds a year – a huge enterprise even by present standards if the changing value of money is taken into account. But Chaplin's actual profit was not so large. Although he died a rich man, most of his fortune came from railway shares.

Chaplin's headquarters was the Swan with Two Necks, though he also operated from several other inns. Sherman's coaches ran from the Bull and Mouth, the greatest of the London coaching inns, and Horne's biggest inn was the Golden Cross, rebuilt several times and finally demolished to make room for Trafalgar Square. (None of the great coaching inns in London has survived to the present.) After the Bull and Mouth, the best-known inn was the Bell Savage, which Robert Nelson took over from Robert Gray when Gray moved to the Bolt-in-tun.

The table shows some of the chief London proprietors in the early 1830s, the inns they worked from and their major coach services.

Many turnpike trusts went bankrupt when they found that the income gained from tolls was not enough to pay their expenses in maintaining the roads. The trusts were always pressing the government for higher tolls, while the coach proprietors, who provided a large part of their income, pressed just as hard for lower tolls.

Certain travellers were excused paying tolls. They included vehicles or riders carrying the mail, transport of materials for mending the roads, priests returning from church, soldiers, and voters on election day. The following table shows the returns from a toll-gate in Essex.

Annual Receipts at Shenfield Toll-gate

1819	£1,983	8	1
1824	1,875	4	5
1830	1,722	17	0
1846	411	8	11

The disastrous fall in 1846 was a result of the opening of the London–Colchester railway in 1843.

PROPRIETOR	INN	MAIL-COACHES	STAGECOACHES
William Chaplin	Swan With Two Necks, Lad Lane White Horse, Fetter Lane Spread Eagle, Gracechurch Street Cross Keys, Gracechurch Street Spread Eagle, Regent's Circus	Bath, Bristol, Devonport, Dover, Holyhead, Hull, Liverpool, Manchester, Norwich via Ipswich, Portsmouth (with Gray), Southampton, Stroud (with Horne), Wells (with Fagg), Yarmouth	Stagecoaches to all parts of the country; Manchester *Defiance*, Newcastle *Highflyer*, etc.
Edward Sherman	Bull and Mouth, St Martin's-le-Grand Oxford Arms, Warwick Lane (freight)	Edinburgh, Exeter, Glasgow, Leeds, Ludlow (via Worcester)	Most parts; fast day-coaches to the north and west especially (Shrewsbury *Wonder*, Manchester *Telegraph*).
William Horne (d. 1828) and Benjamin W. Horne (William's son)	Golden Cross, Charing Cross Cross Keys, Wood Street George and Blue Boar, Holborn	Chester, Dover Foreign, Gloucester, Hastings, Stroud (with Chaplin)	Bedford *Times*, Birmingham *Tally-Ho*, Liverpool *Umpire*: fierce rivalry with Sherman.
Robert Nelson	Bell Savage, Ludgate Hill		Chiefly to the south and west; also Cambridge *Star*, Manchester *Beehive*.
Ann Nelson (Robert's mother)	Bull, Aldgate		Exeter *Defiance* and many East Anglian coaches.

10 TRAVEL BY STAGECOACH

One reason why stage- and mail-coaches travelled so much faster in the nineteenth century was that they changed horses frequently. The average stage in the 1830s was ten to twelve miles, though it varied a great deal. On a long run, like Edinburgh–London, or on a cross-country route, the average stage was usually longer. On short, popular journeys, like London–Brighton (*below*), it was less. Between Bath and

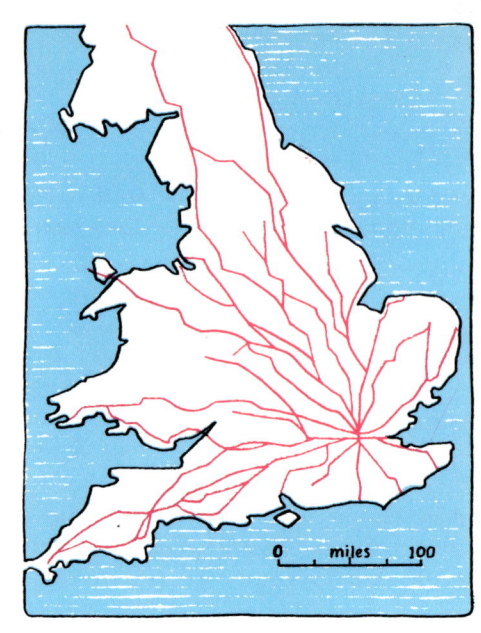

Map of mail-coach routes, 1836. Only the main routes ▶ *from London are shown: there were hundreds of cross-mails also. The long-distance stagecoaches covered much the same routes, and so – unfortunately for the coaching business – did the railways when they were built.*

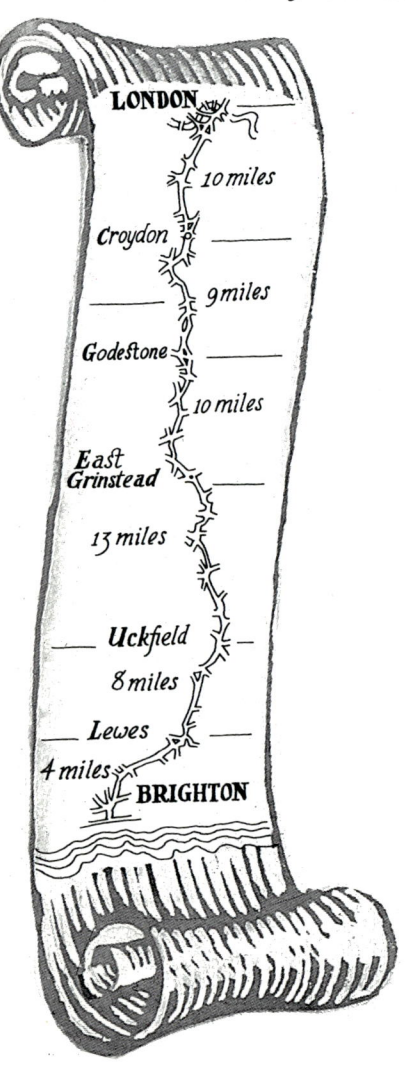

LONDON
10 miles
Croydon
9 miles
Godstone
10 miles
East Grinstead
13 miles
Uckfield
8 miles
Lewes
4 miles
BRIGHTON

Starting a stagecoach service was always a gamble. Would it attract enough fare-paying passengers to make the coach profitable? Many stagecoaches which started hopefully went off the road after a few months because they did not pay. But if a new stagecoach was seen to be a success, it attracted trouble of a different kind: competition.

No one could enforce a monopoly of any route (though Mr Horne of the Golden Cross once put a rival out of business by buying up all the available horses in a certain district), and coach proprietors were

Newbury the average stage was only seven miles, but from Newbury to London, where the country was less hilly, it was nearer ten.

Thanks to the skill and experience of horsekeepers and coachmen, the time taken to change the horses was amazingly short. The rules of the Post Office, which was very strict about keeping time, allowed mail-coaches two minutes for each change, but it was often done in half the time. Looking at the complicated harness on a four-horses team, with its reins, traces, pole chains, splinter bars, and many other parts, this seems almost incredible. But it was done hundreds of times a day.

Travelling by stagecoach was expensive. Poor people could not afford it, and most people travelled only if they had to. The following table[1] shows stagecoach fares from London to Birmingham and to Brighton at various times (fares did not change much over the years, however), together with the railway fare in the year 1860. (It has to be remembered that, besides the fare, coach passengers were expected to tip the coachmen and guards, which added about 20 per cent to their bill. They also had to pay for their meals, which might add another 30 per cent on a long journey.)

		Fare	Railway Fare in 1860	
Birmingham	1776	£1–1–0 (outside 10s 6d)	1st Class	£1–0–0
	1834	£1–0–0 (outside 10s)	2nd Class	15s
			3rd Class	9s 5d
Brighton	1770	14s	1st Class	10s 6d
	1809	£1–3–0 (outside 13s)	2nd Class	8s
	1819	10s (outside 5s)	3rd Class	5s
	1839	£1–0–0 (outside 12s)		

1. Information from Harold W. Hart, *Journal of Transport History*, May 1960.

quick to cash in on the successes of their rivals. When Sherman's Shrewsbury Wonder *proved so popular, Horne put on a rival to run just ahead of the* Wonder. *Sherman retaliated by running a second coach of his own, leaving shortly before Horne's, and when that did not drive his rival off the road he reduced fares on the* Wonder *so sharply that for a time it was running at a heavy loss.*

Another aspect of the fierce competition among rival stagecoaches was the effort of each company to keep a faster time than its rivals. Added to the sporting spirit of coachmen, this resulted in flat-out races between rival coaches on the open road. Racing was forbidden, but some coach proprietors encouraged their coachmen to try to beat the opposition, and there were few coachmen who could resist a challenge when a rival coach came up to overtake. One or two nasty accidents happened as a result of racing.

11 THE PERILS OF COACHING

Coaches had accidents no less often than motor-cars do now and to judge by the many reports of coaching accidents in the newspapers of the time, travelling by stagecoach was a rather dangerous business. Broken bones were quite common, and several of the most famous coachmen died from injuries received in an accident. Inside passengers were safer than outsiders, who could be flung off by a sudden shock and had a long way to fall. However, as a rule, an accident in a coach going at ten or twelve miles an hour, was less serious than an accident in a motor-car going at fifty or sixty.

Accidents usually happened, as they still do, through human carelessness; a worn harness not replaced, an axlebox not oiled, horses left unattended, a driver pulling the wrong rein. But some accidents could not be prevented by the most careful coachman. The driver of an Exeter mail-coach once had the unnerving experience of seeing his horses attacked by a lioness! (She had escaped from a travelling zoo.)

Coaches, even the more low-slung coaches of the nineteenth century, were rather top-heavy, and much the commonest kind of accident was an overturn. If the coach turned too sharply and the wheels locked, if a wheel broke, or came off the axle, or went over a large stone, it might be enough to tip over the coach. One of the most frightening experiences for the traveller was to see the horses bolting, out of the driver's control. They might run for miles before being halted, or they might crash the coach at any moment.

◄ *The coachman's worst enemy was the weather. Guiding a team of four horses along a dark and slippery road on a winter's night with freezing rain blowing into his face was enough to make anyone wish he had taken up a more comfortable profession. But rain, frost, hail, and winds did not stop the stagecoach (though one or two were blown over in high gales). Nor did fog – fog so thick that a man with a flaming torch was hired to walk in front of the coach in city streets. What did stop it was a flood or a heavy snowfall. In the famous snowstorm at Christmas time, 1836, coaches all over England were stuck fast for two days. Not even the mail got through. Floods were just as bad, and more common, because river banks then were not so well-kept, and there were fewer locks, sluices, and dykes. Occasionally, coaches were actually washed away in a flood and their passengers drowned.* ►

▲

Because accidents were so common, or at least seemed so common (people had not grown used to death on the roads and were more shocked by it than they are today), attempts were made to invent a safer coach in the early nineteenth century. Several 'safety' coaches of different kinds appeared on the Brighton road. All had one thing in common: they were designed to be less easily overturned. Bodies were lower, wheels smaller and wider apart, and heavy luggage was not piled on the roof, where it made the coach even more top-heavy. But 'safety' coaches proved to be a passing fashion and soon disappeared. It is hard to see why because, if the reports were true, they really were safer, yet travelled just as fast. Probably the reason is to be found in the conservatism of the coaching business. Coachbuilders were unwilling to change their ideas; coachmen despised anything 'newfangled'; and coach proprietors would not spend money on replacing their coaches with the new 'safety' types. People in the coaching business were proud of their profession, and that kind of pride often breeds a dislike of change.

12 COACHING INNS

The coaching age was also the golden age of the English inn (the word 'hotel' only came in with railways). Coaches started and finished at inns, and the staging posts where they changed horses on the road were usually inns. Passengers could get a meal or a bed for the night; horses could be stabled, post-chaises hired, and connections made with cross-country coaches. Many inns provided private sitting-rooms and a hall for large meetings. Business deals, club meetings, election campaigns, charity dinners – every kind of social activity went on at the inn.

Above: coach passengers at breakfast in the Bull, Red-bourn, a famous inn on the Holyhead Road (A5). The fat and smiling, red-faced landlord welcoming travellers to his dining table loaded with good food is not an imaginary picture. In coaching days inns provided bigger and better meals than at any time before or since. The food was not so very different from the food we eat now, though there was certainly more of it. At a good inn, the travellers would expect to find soup; several kinds of fish including eels and fresh-water fish now seldom seen;

plenty of meat, especially mutton and beef, and probably chicken or game, including venison (but fewer vegetables than would be served now); plum pudding, fruit pies, custard, and trifle, fruit and cheese. The price of such a meal was about four shillings. The food was usually all placed on the table together, though meat and vegetables were eaten separately. Of course, simpler places provided simpler meals, and some people preferred to buy their dinner at a 'take-away' cook shop, where roast meat, a bottle of strong beer, and a bread roll cost about a shilling and you could take as much meat as you liked.

A big coaching inn was a busy and profitable establishment. The Bull and Mouth in St Martin's-le-Grand, the Euston station of the coaching age, had more than twenty coaches leaving for the north and west every day, and the same number arriving. Most inns were built around a courtyard. Galleries ran around the sides and an archway led into the street. On the ground floor were a ticket office and waiting room, a coffee room, and stairways leading to the galleries. Horses in the London inns were often stabled underground: there was room for 200 at the Swan with Two Necks in Lad Lane (now Gresham Street), the headquarters of William Chaplin. Big coaching inns also kept a room specially for their coachmen, who sometimes invited privileged travellers to join them for a drink.

Most English inns still take pride in their signboards, which often commemorate the old coaching days when inns were so prosperous. There are hundreds of pubs in England called the Coach and Horses and many more, like the Red Rover, the Regent, or the Falcon, are named after stagecoaches that once changed horses there.

The names of some of the old inns are rather mysterious. The first sign of the Goose and Gridiron in St Paul's Churchyard was meant to show a swan and a lyre, the badge of the Musicians' Society. Ordinary people thought it looked more like a goose and a gridiron, and that was what it became. The Bull and Mouth was originally the Boulogne Mouth, named in honour of King Henry VIII's capture of Boulogne harbour (or 'mouth') in 1544. The Belle Sauvage (another famous London coaching inn) was first called the Bell, and the Savage was added when a Mrs Savage became proprietor in the sixteenth century. But in the eighteenth century the inn's sign showed a wild man (or 'savage') standing by a bell. Then someone decided that 'Bell Savage' must be badly spelled French, so the inn became the Belle Sauvage (beautiful savage).

The 'diligence', which looked very like the later omnibus, could be seen on the streets before the end of the eighteenth century. It was a light van, drawn by a pair or three horses at walking pace. Such vehicles were more common in France than in Britain, and took their name from the ▶ French diligence.

George Shillibeer's omnibus carried twenty-two passengers on bench seats along the sides. It was drawn by three horses abreast and ran a regular service to Paddington from the City. Shillibeer had two of these vehicles, one called the Omnibus (like the diligence, the name came from France, where omnibuses were already running) and the other named after himself. Strangely, it was the name 'shillibeer' that was then often used to describe the type of vehicle, but 'omnibus' soon replaced it, and people finally settled for the shorter 'bus'. Shillibeer's omnibuses were popular, but they were too large for the streets of those days and the next generation of horse-omnibuses were smaller, seating twelve inside. ▼

OMNIBUS

13 OMNIBUS AND STEAM COACH

Stage- and mail-coaches travelled long distances, from 50 to 400 miles. On shorter journeys, between towns and suburbs, different vehicles were used. For every stagecoach that left London bound for places like Bristol, Shrewsbury or Norwich, dozens of 'short-stages' left for Richmond, Uxbridge or Barnet, an hour or two's drive from the West End. The 'short-stage' was often a retired stagecoach, or an old private carriage. It was drawn by a pair of horses only, and therefore demanded none of the driving skill of the four-horse coach. It was usually rather shabby, crowded, and slow – certainly not a glamorous vehicle like its long-distance cousins. The big London coach proprietors would not operate such vehicles, which they regarded as dirty little mongrels obstructing the splendid progress of their thoroughbreds. All the same, the short-stage provided a valuable service for people travelling to the suburbs.

In city centres, public transport was hardly necessary before the eighteenth century because cities were small enough for most people to walk. London was an exception, but London was much larger than any other city in Europe. The increase of hackney cabs showed that the need for city transport was growing, but hackney cabs were expensive. Cheap city transport (cheap by the standards of the time, when all travel was expensive) began in 1829, when George Shillibeer put his omnibus on the London streets.

Several people experimented with steam-driven road vehicles in the eighteenth century. Goldsworthy Gurney, a rich West Countryman, made several steam-coaches in the 1820s. One ran between Gloucester and Cheltenham for a few months in 1831. Walter Hancock's most famous steam-coach, or steam-omnibus, was the Enterprise, *which appeared in London in 1833. It could do 20 m.p.h., or so Hancock said, and carried fourteen passengers between Paddington and the City.*

The steam-coach was one of those good ideas that just do not work. There were many reasons. In the first place, steam-coaches were hated by too many people. Naturally, everyone in the coaching business loathed them, fearing the loss of their jobs. The turnpike trusts accused them of ruining the roads and forced them to pay enormous

tolls at the toll-gates. Gravel roads, even macadamized, were not smooth enough for steam-coaches: the jolting caused broken steam pipes and cracked pistons. With their tenders of coke and tanks of water, steam-coaches were very heavy. They were also noisy, smoky, smelly, and – if the boiler burst, as sometimes happened – dangerous. Country gentlemen disliked them because they frightened horses and disturbed the game. They had to stop to take on water nearly as often as stage-coaches stopped to change horses, and they did not go very much faster – not in safety at any rate. Although steamrollers and steam traction engines lived on for many years into the age of the motor-car, no country in the world adopted steam road vehicles as a normal method of transport. Railways proved to be the answer.

The last Newcastle mail-coach rolled sadly through the city on 5 July 1847. Coachmen and guard wore black bands of mourning, and the coach flew the Union flag at half-mast. Along the road flags on the buildings were lowered in sympathy. People recognized that a glorious institution was passing away. But they preferred to travel by train.

The *Shrewsbury* Wonder *was one of the most famous stagecoaches in England. It was the first fast day-coach, put on by Edward Sherman in 1825. Leaving the Bull and Mouth 6.30 a.m. it reached Shrewsbury, 158 miles away, at 10.30 p.m., keeping an average speed of almost twelve miles an hour (not counting halts). When the London–Birmingham Railway opened in 1838, the* Wonder *tried to compete with it, and one famous day it left London at the same time as the train and arrived in Birmingham first. But it could not keep up such a pace. Soon afterwards it suffered the grave indignity of travelling on a railway truck on the London to Birmingham stretch of its journey: then, as customers dwindled, the* Wonder *was taken off the road for good.*
▼

Railway lines in Britain in 1845. Fifteen years after the opening of the Manchester–Liverpool Railway, nearly every major coaching road in England was duplicated by a railway line.
▼

14 THE END OF AN AGE

Stagecoaches did not reach their peak of speed and efficiency until the 1820s. Less than twenty years later, they were in rapid decline. In 1838 the income from tolls fell sharply, and it soon sank even farther. The toll-gates rusted on their hinges, the toll-houses were deserted, and the roads began to fall back into the state from which the turnpike trusts had rescued them. Along the road, the smart coaching inns faded into cheap pubs, or closed down altogether. The price of horses fell and old coachmen hung about the deserted inn-yards hoping for odd jobs.

The reason for this decline was simple. Railways put an end to the long-distance stagecoach. Travel by train was much faster, cheaper, and more comfortable. The coaching world might say that railways were dangerous, dirty, and (because they needed special tracks) absurdly expensive. But the coach did not stand a chance in competition with them.

Of course, it was only the long-distance coaches on the main roads that suffered. Horse-drawn

The first public railway in Britain, between Stockton and Darlington, opened in 1825. The plan was to use horses to draw the carriages along the rails, but George Stephenson, the engineer, persuaded the Company that a steam locomotive would do the job better. His Locomotion No. 1 became the first engine to work on a public railway.

The Stockton–Darlington Railway was intended mainly for goods, but rail passenger service began in earnest with the opening of the Manchester–Liverpool line in 1830. At the beginning of that year there were twenty-two public coaches running daily between Manchester and Birmingham. By the end of the year, five trains were running and only four coaches.

vehicles were still needed in country districts and they increased hugely in Victorian towns, where they provided the only form of transport until the tram and the motor bus. But the crack stagecoaches like the Manchester *Telegraph* and the Birmingham *Tally-Ho* were gone for ever. The whole splendid scene disappeared in a great puff of railway smoke.

SOME COACHING LANGUAGE

Drag: a coach, especially a private, four-horse coach.

Dragsman, also *coachie, whip:* coachman.

Spoon: a bad coachman.

Shooter: a guard.

Ribbons: reins.

Tool: whip.

Tommy: a thick-thonged whip used by old-fashioned coachmen who depended on violence to keep their horses moving.

Yard of tin: coach horn.

Benjamin: a heavy topcoat with several layers over the shoulders, worn by coachmen.

Cattle: the horses.

Miller: a horse likely to kick.

Raker: an unreliable, fretful horse.

Three blind 'uns and a bolter: a very bad team (not meant literally).

Parliamentary horse: a horse that trotted as fast as others galloped; galloping was banned by act of parliament, but as long as one of the four horses was trotting the coach was within the law.

Springing the team: putting the horses into a gallop.

Hung up: brought to a sudden stop by some mishap.

Feather-edging: driving too near the kerb on corners.

Bringing it home in a sack: an expression implying that the coach was so badly damaged by kicks from the horse that it was smashed to pieces (not meant literally!).

Up: towards London.

Down: away from London.

Ground: the road covered by the coach; thus *higher ground* (near London), *middle ground,* and *lower ground.*

Both sides of the road: to and from; a coachman who drove to any place 'both sides of the road' drove there and back again.

Mad woman: an empty coach.

Butterfly: a coach that ran in the summer only.

Shouldering: the practice of picking up a passenger on the road, usually for a short distance, without entering his name on the waybill; the fare being pocketed by the coachman.

Short one: a passenger not named on the waybill (see *Shouldering*).

Kicking: dunning passengers for a tip.

A nice piece of muslin: a pretty girl.

A flash of lightning: a strong drink.

Grog-blossom: redness of face, caused by drinking grog (rum and water).

Gammon: false show, affectation; hence 'gammonacious', favourite adjective of Mr Jorrocks (the fox-hunting grocer in Surtees's novels), meaning 'phoney'.

All illustrations are based on contemporary sources. Original material reproduced is as follows: coaching bills (spreads 1 & 2) and 'Breakfast at Bull Inn, Redbourn' by James Pollard (spread 12) are from Margetson, Journey by Stages, London 1967; *John Palmer (spread 2),* National Portrait Gallery; *William Chaplin (spread 9),* Radio Times Hulton Picture Library.